FOUL-MOUTHED PETS

**Mike Lepine &
Mark Leigh**

summersdale

FOUL-MOUTHED PETS

First published in 2007 under a different title

Summersdale Publishers Ltd
46 West Street
Chichester
West Sussex
PO19 1RP
UK

www.summersdale.com

Printed and bound in China

ISBN: 978-1-84953-277-8

Substantial discounts on bulk quantities of Summersdale books are available to corporations, professional associations and other organisations. For details telephone Summersdale Publishers on (+44-1243-771107), fax (+44-1243-786300) or email (nicky@summersdale.com).

For Zippy, the rudest cat in the history of cats

And also Maxwell Woofington III, he's not
rude although he is a cocker spaniel

Thank yous

The authors would like to thank the following people for their assistance and tolerance: Philippa Hatton-Lepine, Gage Hatton-Lepine, Rob Shreeve, Debbie Leigh, Polly & Barney Leigh (kids – don't ever read this book) and Robert Day – who wanted to be mentioned in a tasteful and sophisticated work of literature.

Meet the authors

Mike Lepine and Mark Leigh have had over forty humour/trivia books published including three number one best-sellers. Celebrities they have worked with include Adrian Edmondson, Julian Clary, Des Lynam, Jeremy Beadle, Roy Chubby Brown, Chris Tarrant and Rolf Harris.

They have also written and developed numerous TV programmes and recently completed their first comedy film screenplay.

www.summersdale.com

@SummersdaleLOL